BE AI SAVVY

UNDERSTANDING THE PROS AND CONS OF ARTIFICIAL INTELLIGENCE

by Tammy Enz

CAPSTONE PRESS
a capstone imprint

Published by Capstone Press, an imprint of Capstone
1710 Roe Crest Drive, North Mankato, Minnesota 56003
capstonepub.com

Library of Congress Cataloging-in-Publication Data is available on the Library of Congress website.

ISBN: 9798875253928 (hardcover)
ISBN: 9798875253874 (paperback)
ISBN: 9798875253881 (ebook PDF)

Summary: From deepfake videos to chatbots that sound just like humans, AI is more powerful than ever. But with great power comes great responsibility! In this must-read book, young readers will learn how to think critically about AI-generated content, protect personal information, and separate fact from fiction. Discover the pros and cons of AI, from its ability to solve big problems to the risks of misinformation.

Editorial Credits:
Editor: Donald Lemke; Designer: Bobbie Nuytten; Media Researcher: Svetlana Zhurkin; Production Specialist: Whitney Schaefer

Image Credits:
Getty Images: baloon111, 15, bombermoon, 27, Capuski, 25, eclipse_images, cover (middle), Images By Tang Ming Tung, 23, Ismagilov, 19, Marcus Lindstrom, 14, mikimad, 29, portishead1, 22, shironosov, 4; Shutterstock: Antlii, 21, Best-Backgrounds (computer code), cover and throughout, Deemerwha studio, 6, DIA TV, 11, fizkes, 20, Frame Stock Footage, 8, 9, Gorodenkoff, 10, Julia Zavalishina, 18, LightField Studios, 17, Linaimages, 13, Mongta Studio, 24, Rawpixel, 16, Scharfsinn, 7, SkillUp, cover (top) and throughout, Tada Images, 5, Tero Vesalainen, 12

Printed and bound in China. PO 6459

Table of Contents

CHAPTER 1

Our AI World

Have you ever played a video game that seemed to know exactly what move you'd make next? Or watched a video online that felt like it was made just for you? Maybe you've even read something that sounded real but wasn't. That's all thanks to artificial intelligence, or AI.

AI is everywhere, from voice assistants that answer your questions to apps that recommend music and movies. But how do you know if AI is safe to use? And how can you make sure you're in control—not the other way around?

Discover how to recognize AI, use it wisely, and stay safe. AI can be useful, but it's important to understand how it works and how to spot its tricks.

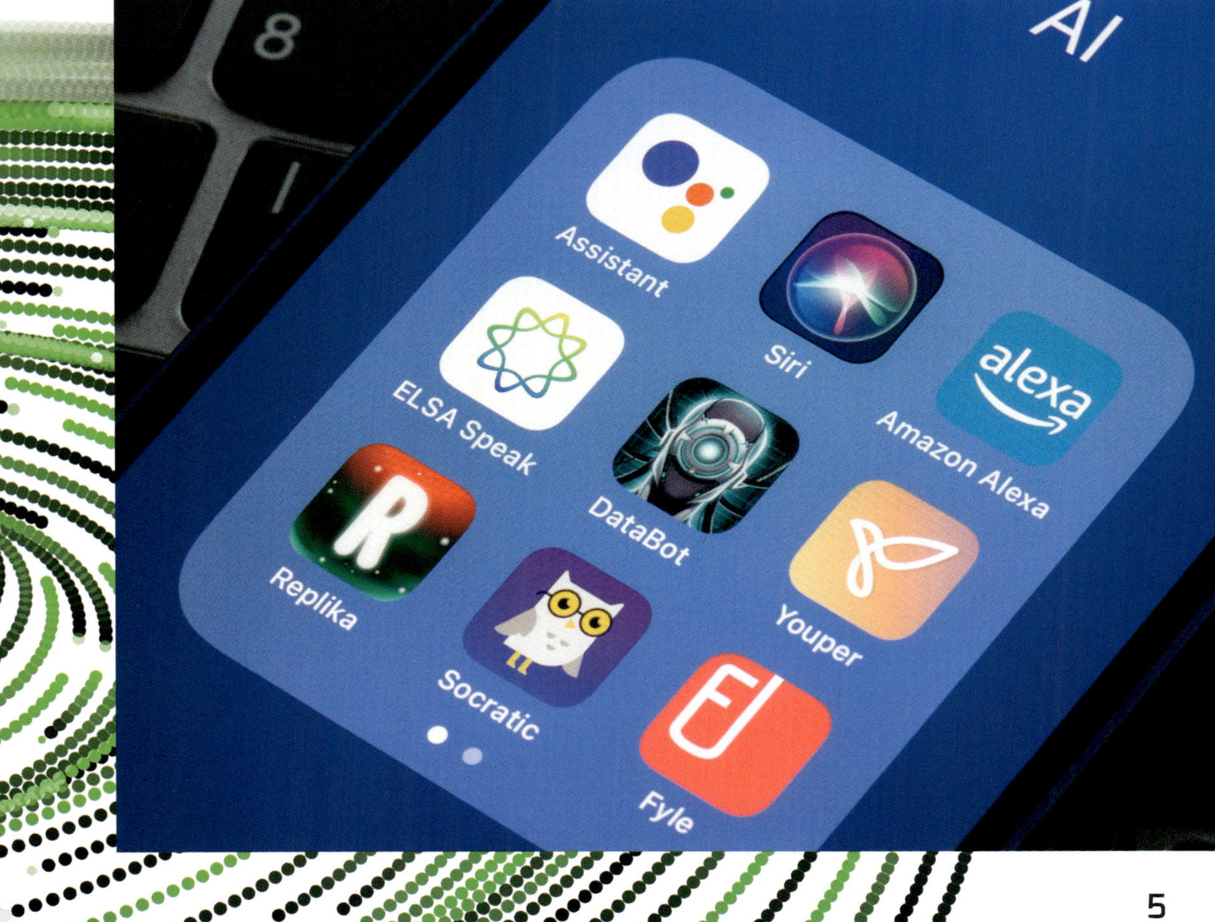

AI is great at analyzing data. It looks at large amounts of information, identifies patterns, and makes predictions. This helps apps and devices work smarter, faster, and in ways that feel more personal to you.

Everyday AI Technologies

Voice assistants—Siri, Alexa, and Google Assistant use AI to understand your words and provide helpful answers.

Video games—AI controls how game characters react and move, making the experience more exciting.

Smart apps—Ever noticed Netflix or YouTube suggesting videos based on what you've watched? AI predicts what you'll like next.

Self-driving cars—AI helps cars detect roads, signs, and obstacles to drive without a person at the wheel.

AI doesn't just analyze information. This technology can create things too, like stories, artwork, and music. Instead of simply recommending content, AI tools can generate completely original images, text, and even videos.

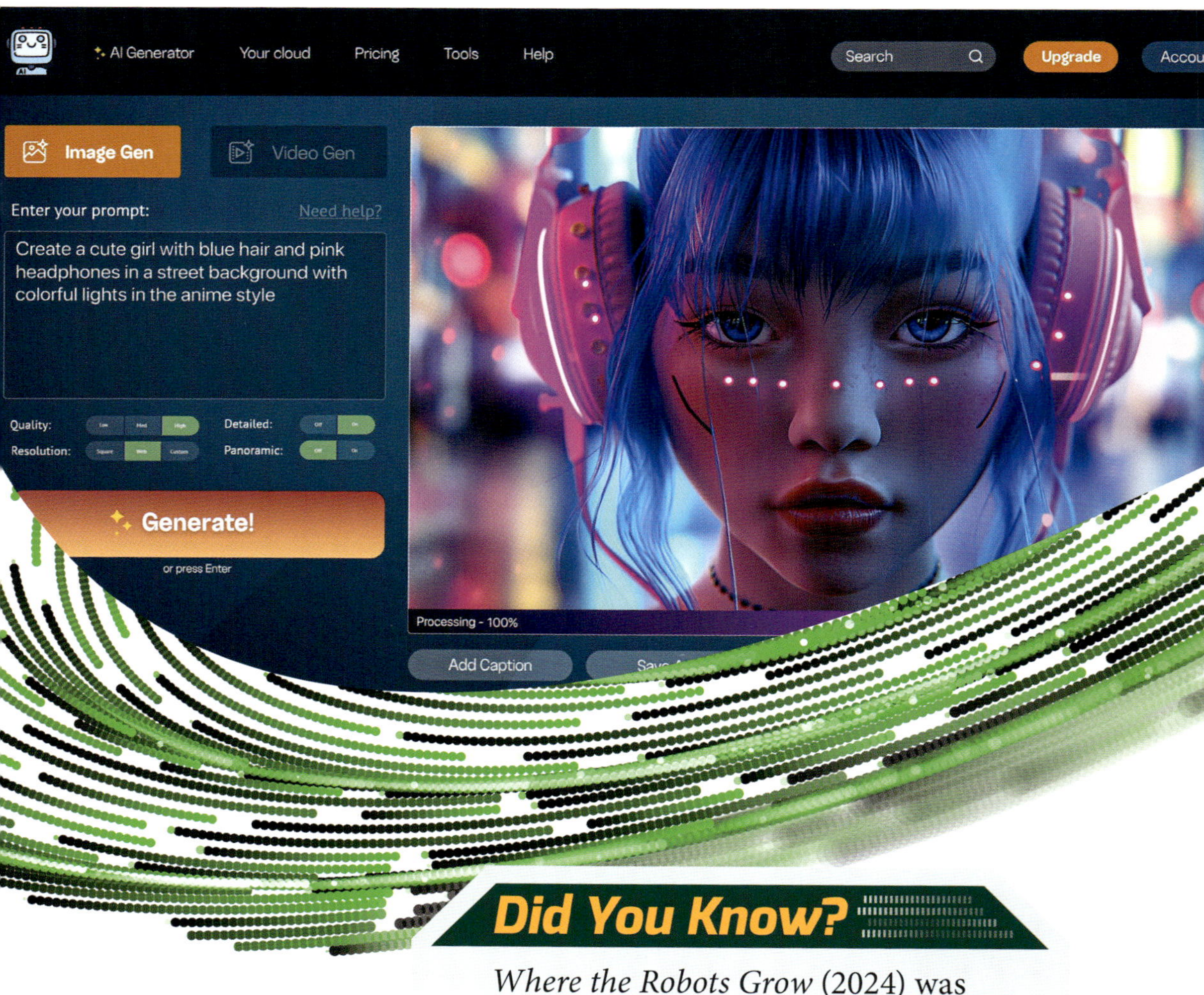

Did You Know?

Where the Robots Grow (2024) was the first fully AI-generated animated movie!

Creating AI Content

AI writing assistants—AI-powered programs can help write essays, poems, and even full books by predicting words and ideas based on past writing.

AI art and images—Some AI tools can generate pictures from text descriptions called prompts. Type “a cat singing on stage,” and AI will create that image.

AI-generated movies and videos—Some films and animations are made entirely by AI, with no human artists or animators involved.

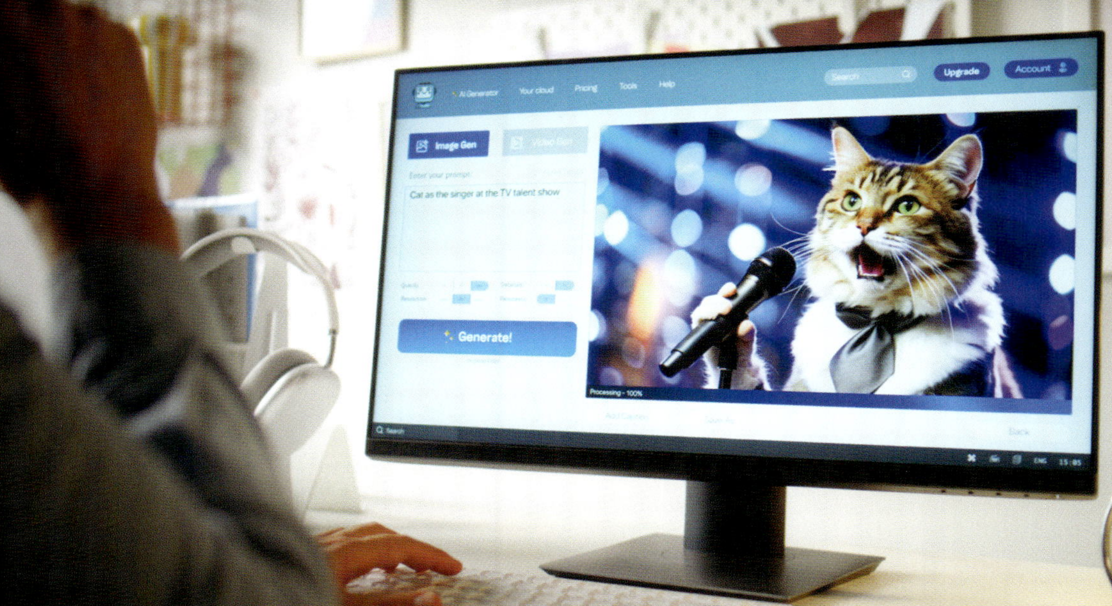

CHAPTER 2

Spotting AI in the Wild

Many experts believe that 90 percent of online content will be AI-generated in the near future. That means much of what you see and hear—videos, photos, news stories, and even voices—could be created by AI instead of a real person.

Some AI-generated content is easy to spot, like video game characters or virtual assistants. But AI can also create incredibly real content that can make you believe something that isn't true.

Examples of AI-generated content you might find online:

- Fake news articles designed to spread false information.
- AI-edited photos that look real but contain seemingly impossible details.
- AI-generated music that copies real artists.
- Chatbots that pose as real people in online conversations.

While some AI-generated content is harmless—like funny filters or animated characters—others can be misleading. That's why learning to spot AI in the wild is more important than ever.

Have you ever seen a video of a famous person saying something shocking . . . only to find out it wasn't real? That might have been a deepfake. These AI-generated videos swap faces, copy voices, and create entirely fake events.

Deepfake technology studies thousands of real images and videos to build a digital version of someone's face and voice. While deepfakes can be fun, they can also be used to spread false information and trick people.

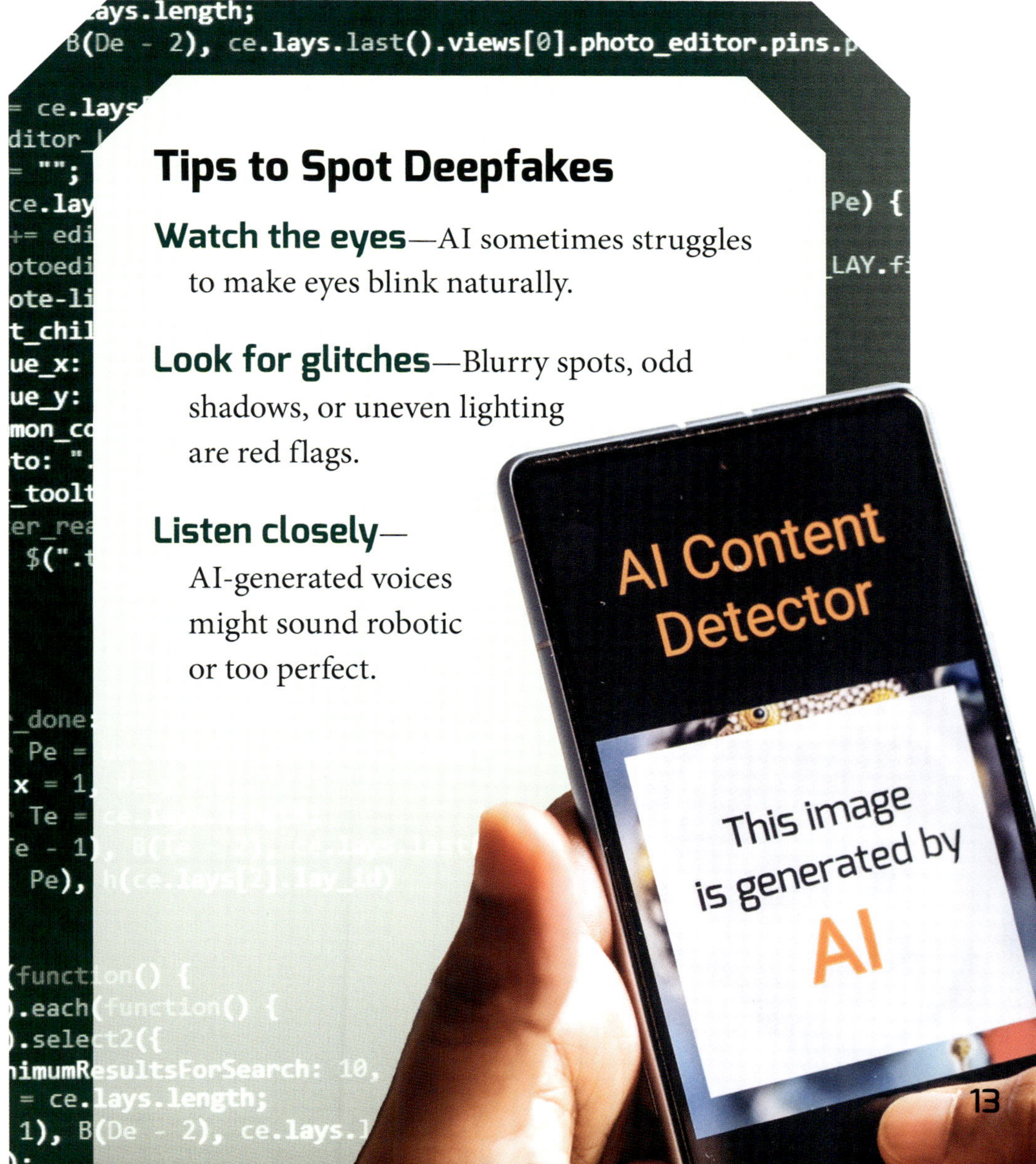

Tips to Spot Deepfakes

Watch the eyes—AI sometimes struggles to make eyes blink naturally.

Look for glitches—Blurry spots, odd shadows, or uneven lighting are red flags.

Listen closely—AI-generated voices might sound robotic or too perfect.

Even if a photo or video looks real, that doesn't mean it is. AI can generate fake news, edit photos, and even create entire conversations that never happened. That's why it's important to think critically about what you see online.

Be a Digital Detective

Check the source—Real news has links to trusted websites or journalists. If there's no author or source, be suspicious.

Look for mistakes—AI struggles with details like hand movements, extra fingers, or unnatural blinking.

Use fact-checking websites—Sites like Snopes.com and FactCheck.org can help confirm whether something is real.

Ever noticed how TikTok, Instagram, or YouTube seem to “know” what you like? That’s AI at work! These sites track what you watch, like, and share to suggest videos, posts, and even friends based on your interests.

AI can make social media more fun, but it can also spread false information without people realizing it. Some AI-generated posts, photos, and videos look real but are completely fake. These fakes can trick people into believing something untrue.

Stay Smart on Social Media

Check the source—Who posted it? Is it from a trusted news organization or a random account?

Watch out for misleading ads—Some AI-created posts are designed to sell products or push false stories. Avoid clicking these links before asking an adult.

Think before sharing—If a post seems shocking or too weird to be true, double-check before spreading it.

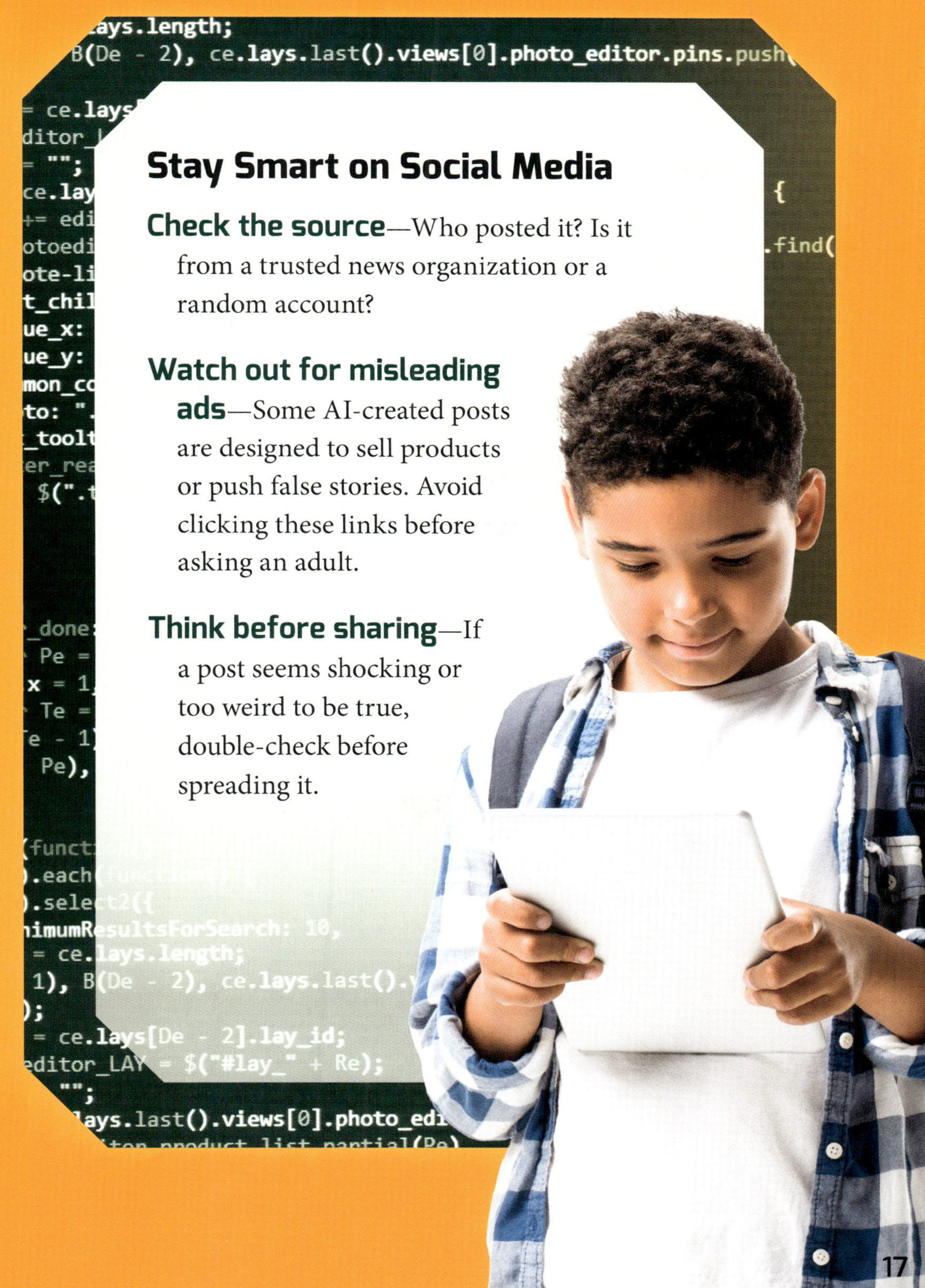

CHAPTER 3

Using AI Responsibly

AI can be fun and helpful, but it's important to keep your personal information private. Many AI tools collect data—like your name, favorite things, and even your location. This data can be stored and used in ways you might not expect, such as advertising, recommendations, or tracking.

AI often profiles users, meaning it learns your habits and suggests content based on your interests. While this can be useful, it can also limit what you see by only showing you things AI thinks you'll like.

Did You Know?

Some AI-powered apps track your location to suggest places to visit—but that also means companies can see where you go.

Would you share your password with a stranger? Probably not! But when you use AI-powered tools, it's just as important to protect your information from hackers and data tracking.

Did You Know?

More than two-thirds of people use the same password for multiple accounts—making it easier for hackers to guess.

Keep Your Information Safe

Don't share passwords—Even if an AI chatbot asks, never give out login details.

Think before you share—Does AI really need your name, age, or location? Avoid sharing this information online.

Use privacy settings—Many apps let you limit what AI can access. Adjust these settings for more control. Get a trusted adult to help you if you're unsure how to make these changes.

Being smart about online safety means knowing when to say no to AI requests. If you're ever unsure, ask an adult before sharing anything sensitive.

AI can be a great learning tool, but it's important to use it the right way. AI can help with math problems, essays, and even learning new languages. But it shouldn't do the work for you!

Think of AI as a teammate, not a replacement for your own thinking. If you let AI do everything, you will miss out on learning important skills.

Use AI Wisely for Schoolwork

Use AI for ideas—AI can help brainstorm topics but shouldn't write assignments for you. Remember, teachers use tools to check for AI-generated work!

Check AI-generated answers—AI sometimes gets things wrong or makes things up, so double-check facts with trusted sources.

Understand, don't just copy—AI might explain things in a simpler way, but you should still make sure you truly understand.

AI isn't just for school—it can also be used for creativity, fun, and making the world a better place! AI tools help people with disabilities, translate languages, create digital art, and even help scientists solve big problems.

Did You Know?

Scientists and researchers use AI to protect endangered animals by tracking their movements and safeguarding their habitats!

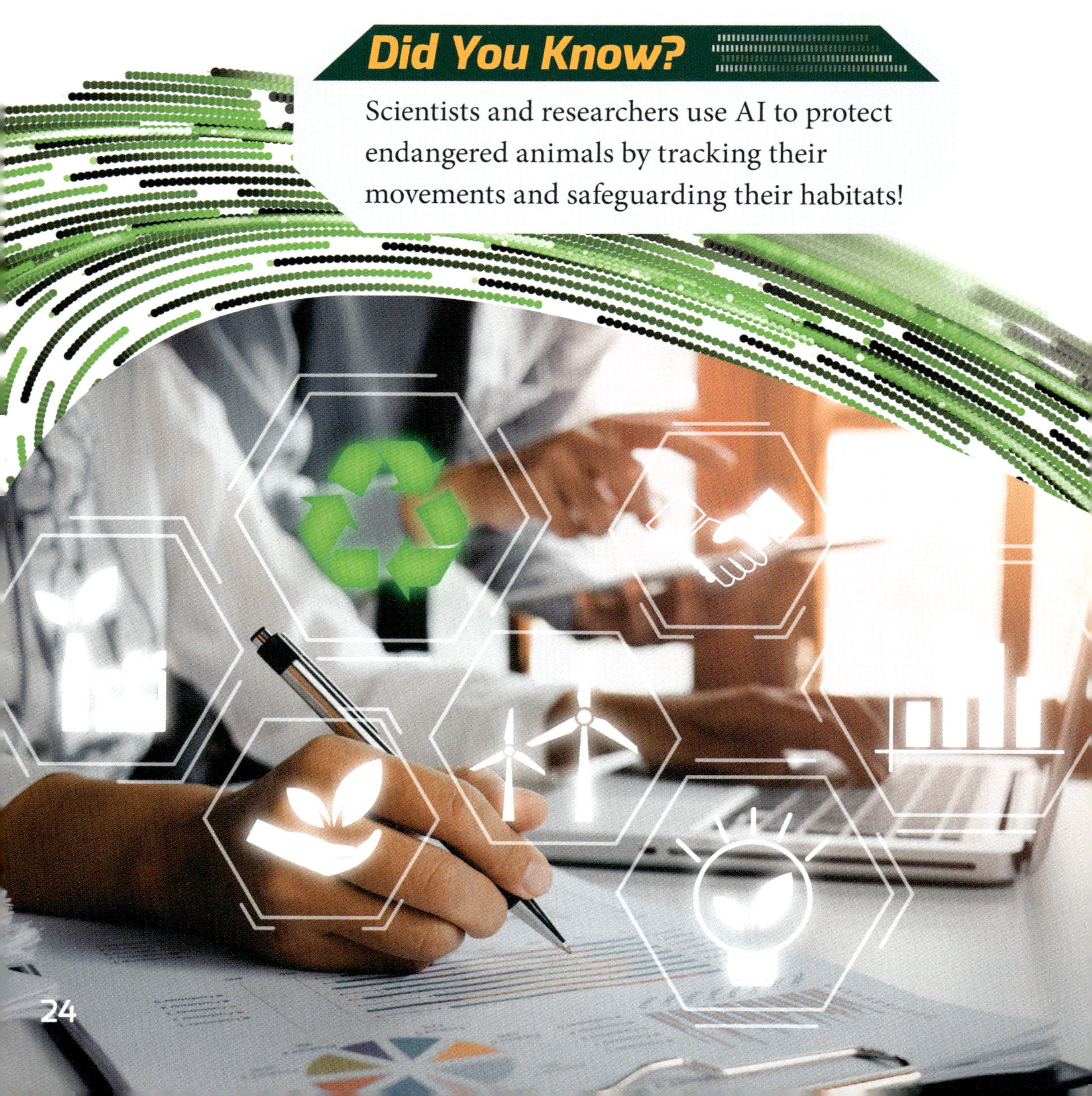

Using AI Responsibly

Double-check your facts—AI isn't perfect, so always verify its answers.

Stay informed—Keep up with how AI is changing so you can use it wisely.

Be kind online—AI helps connect people, but it's important to use it respectfully and not spread misinformation.

Use AI to be creative—Try AI-generated art, music, or coding projects to explore new ideas.

AI is a powerful tool, but how you use it matters. When used responsibly, it can be an amazing way to learn, create, and connect!

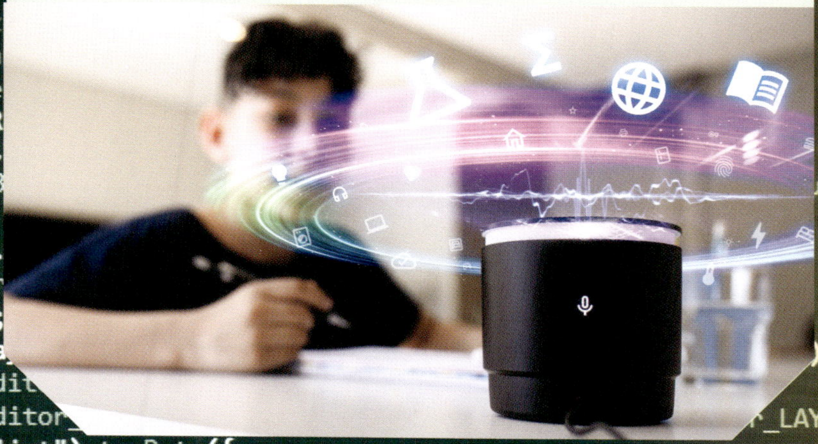

CHAPTER 4

The Good and the Bad

AI is changing the way we learn, create, and interact with technology. It can be a helpful tool but, like anything, it has both pros and cons.

The Good:

- AI can make learning easier by helping with research, writing, and even tutoring in math or language.
- AI provides new forms of entertainment, from video game characters to AI-generated music and personalized playlists.
- AI can help people explore creativity, turning ideas into digital paintings, stories, and even movies.
- Scientists use AI to solve big problems, like predicting storms, protecting endangered animals, and even helping doctors detect diseases early.

Did You Know?

AI is even used in space exploration to help astronauts analyze planets and plan missions!

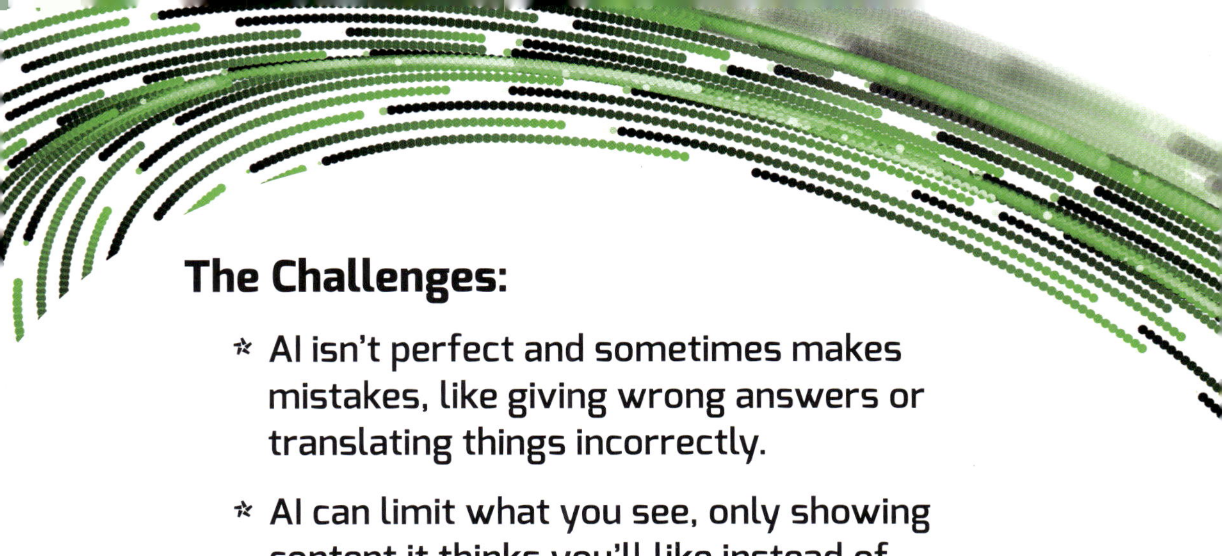

The Challenges:

- AI isn't perfect and sometimes makes mistakes, like giving wrong answers or translating things incorrectly.
- AI can limit what you see, only showing content it thinks you'll like instead of exposing you to new ideas.
- AI can be used to spread false information, like deepfakes or misleading news articles.

AI is here to stay, and it will continue evolving in ways we can't even imagine! The most important thing is to use AI thoughtfully and responsibly.

Here's how you can stay ahead in the world of AI:

Double-check AI-generated content—Don't believe everything AI says or creates.

Stay informed—Keep up with new AI trends and learn how it's changing the world.

Use AI for good—Explore how AI can help with school, creativity, and making a difference.

Think critically—AI is a tool, but you are in charge of how you use it!

From writing stories to solving big problems, AI can be a powerful tool for learning, creativity, and discovery. The future of AI is exciting, but the most important intelligence will always be your own!

Key AI Search Terms

1. AI for Kids
2. Artificial Intelligence Education
3. AI Learning Tools
4. AI in School
5. AI for Social Media Safety
6. AI and Privacy for Children
7. AI and Online Safety

Internet Sites

Britannica Kids: Artificial Intelligence
kids.britannica.com/kids/article/artificial-intelligence/390648

Code.org: Learning for Ages 5 to 11
code.org/student/elementary

ISTE: Artificial Intelligence in Education
iste.org/ai

Glossary

artificial intelligence (ahr-tuh-FISH-uhl in-TEHL-uh-juhns)—computers or robots that can think, learn, and solve problems like people

critical thinking (KRIH-tih-kuhl THING-king)—thinking carefully about something to decide if it's right or wrong

detect (deh-TEKT)—to notice or find something, like figuring out if information is true or fake

generated (JEN-uh-ray-ted)—made or created by something, like a computer making a picture or story

privacy (PRY-vuh-see)—the quality or state of being out of the sight and hearing of other people and keeping personal information safe

responsible (ree-SPON-suh-buhl)—doing the right thing and being careful, like using computers in a safe and smart way

source (SORSS)—the place where information comes from, like a person or website that shares facts

Index

About the Author

Tammy Enz holds a bachelor's degree in civil engineering and a master's degree in journalism and mass communications. She works as a structural engineer and teaches at the University of Wisconsin-Platteville. She has written dozens of books on science and engineering topics for young people.